FUN FAX ™

Jokes, jokes and more Jokes

Designed & Illustrated by Barry Green

Compiled by Rosy Border

ISBN 0-590-20844-6

Copyright © 1990 by Henderson Publishing Limited. All rights reserved.
Published by Scholastic Inc., 555 Broadway, New York, NY 10012,
by arrangement with Henderson Publishing Limited.

12 11 10 9 8 7 6 5 4 3 2 1   4 5 6 7 8 9/9

Printed in Great Britain. First Scholastic printing, October 1994

SCHOLASTIC INC. New York Toronto London Auckland Sydney

LIBRARY

THE LASER by Ray Gunn

DENTISTRY by Phil Macavity

SCHOOL DINNERS by R.E. Volting

SILVER WEDDING by Ann E. Versary

TEATIME by Roland Butta

THE STUPID STRIKER by Mr Goal

TAPE RECORDERS by Cass Ette

WARM CLOTHES by Jack Ette

YOU TOO CAN BE RICH by Robin Banks

ADIOS by C.U. Later

CROSS THE ROAD by Luke Bothways

HELPING OTHERS! by Ada Charity

FALLING by Mr Step

LOVE YOUR MICROWAVE by Andy Gadget

SPLASH! By Eileen Dover

OLD FURNITURE by Anne Teak

SHHH

CALL FOR HELP by Linda Hand

DOGS by K. Nine

THE WINNER! by Vic Torius

TIME FOR SCHOOL by R.U. Upjohn

BELLRINGING FOR BEGINNERS by Paula Rope

BRICKS AND MORTAR by Bill Ding

SERGEANT MAJOR by Reggie Mental

MUSICAL MADNESS

Harry: Did you hear they dug up Mozart's grave?
Garry: Really?
Harry: Yes. He was decomposing!

Tuner: I've come to tune your piano.
Mr. Smith: But I didn't send for you.
Tuner: No, your neighbors did.

Dan: What's the best birthday present for a little boy?
Stan: Well, a drum takes a lot of beating!

What's musical and very useful in a supermarket?
A Chopin Liszt.

And what key is the most important to good manners?
B Natural.

KNOCK KNOCK!

WHO'S THERE?

COW'S GO!

COW'S GO WHO?

OWL'S GO WHO — COW'S GO MOO!

Knock knock!
Who's there?
Hatch!
Hatch who?
That's a nasty cold you've got!

Knock knock!
Who's there?
Tamara!
Tamara who?
Tamara is another day!

Knock knock!
Who's there?
Major!
Major who?
Major answer the door!

Knock knock!
Who's there?
Juno!
Juno who?
Juno what time it is?

KNOCK KNOCK!

WHO'S THERE?

BOO!

BOO WHO?

STOP CRYING!!!

Knock knock!
Who's there?
Roland!
Roland who?
Roland butter, please!

Knock knock!
Who's there?
Tish!
Tish who?
Bless you!

Knock knock!
Who's there?
Carmen!
Carmen who?
Carmen get it!

Knock knock!
Who's there?
Yah!
Yah who?
Ride 'em, cowboy!

KNOCK KNOCK!
WHO'S THERE?
PUDDING!
PUDDING WHO?
PUDDING ON YOUR SHOES BEFORE YOUR PANTS IS A BAD IDEA!

Knock knock!
Who's there?
Cook!
Cook who?
Stop doing bird imitations and open the door!

Knock knock!
Who's there?
Howard!
Howard who?
Howard you like to know?

Knock knock!
Who's there?
Honeydew!
Honeydew who?
Honeydew you want to come out tonight?

Knock knock!
Who's there?
Ida!
Ida who?
Ida terrible time getting here!

COPS & ROBBERS

A policeman saw a little girl walking along the street dragging an old scrubbing brush on a piece of string.

"Nice dog you've got there, kid," said the kindly policeman, stooping to pat the brush.

The little girl gave him a dirty look.

"That isn't a dog!" she said. "It's an old scrubbing brush!"

"Sorry," said the embarrassed policeman, and walked on.

As soon as he had gone the little girl bent down and stroked the brush. "That fooled him, didn't it, Fido!" she said.

News: The artist who has been forging Picassos has been sent to prison. Naturally he says he was framed.

———————————

News: Two prisoners have escaped from jail. One is seven feet tall and the other is four foot nine. Police are looking high and low for them.

———————————

What kind of animal does a crook hate the most? A stool pigeon.

Stan: What's that lady policewoman doing up a tree?
Dan: She's working for the Special Branch.

Who never minds being interrupted in the middle of a sentence?

A CONVICT!

Stan: The police are looking for a crook with one eye called Murphy.
Dan: What's his other eye called?

I SENTENCE YOU TO 50 YEARS IN JAIL!

BUT I'LL NEVER LIVE THAT LONG!

NEVER MIND, JUST DO WHAT YOU CAN!

What do you call a person who breaks into a shop and steals all the pork?

A hamburglar.

And what do thieves eat for dinner? Cheeseburglars.

Why hasn't anyone ever stolen a canal?
It has too many locks.

Policeman: Sorry, son, you'll need a permit to fish here.
Harry: No thanks, I'm doing pretty well with a worm.

Who was the biggest robber in history?
Atlas — he held up the world.

Two convicts were making license plates in prison.
"I shouldn't be here," said one. "I committed the perfect bank robbery, got $100,000 then I made my big mistake."
"What did you do wrong?"
"I stayed to count the money."

Dolly: If I dug a hole in the middle of the park, what would come up?
Polly: Probably a policeman.

HORSE LAUGHS

WHAT HAS 4 LEGS, EATS HAY, AND SEES JUST AS WELL FROM EITHER END?

I DUNNO

A HORSE WITH ITS EYES SHUT!

The Thunder God went for a ride
Upon his favorite filly.
"I'm Thor!" he cried - the horse replied,
"You forgot your thaddle, thilly!"

Why did the pony take throat lozenges?
Because he was a little hoarse.

How do you hire a horse?
Put a brick under each foot.

Garry: Dad, do you water a horse when he's thirsty?
Dad: Yes, that's right.
Garry: Then I'm going to the kitchen to milk the cat!

Why did the farmer call his horse Blacksmith?
The horse kept making a bolt for the door!

WHERE DOES A SICK HORSE GO?

HORSPITAL!

NOT NICE

Hickory Dickory Dock,
Two mice ran up the clock.
The clock struck one
But the other escaped with only minor injuries.

BONG!

"Good news, fellas," shouted the overseer of the
Roman galley. "Double rations today!"
Eagerly the slaves ate their meal.
"Now for the bad news," said the overseer. "The
captain wants to go water-skiing!"

IS YOUR DOG FOND OF CHILDREN?

WELL, YES, BUT HE PREFERS DOG FOOD

Question: When is it bad luck to have a black cat
follow you around?
Answer: When you're a mouse!

Mother: Son, everytime you misbehave,
I get another gray hair.
Son: You must have been a real terror, mom.
Look at Grandma!

Girl: I really hate playing tennis with a
sore loser.
Boy: Oh, I don't know. I'd rather play with a
sore loser than any kind of winner.

Polly: My boyfriend reminds me of the sea.
Dolly: You mean he's wild, restless and
romantic?
Polly: No — he makes me sick.

Harry: When the principal retired from our school
the pupils gave him an illuminated address.
Garry: How lovely. How did they manage that?
Harry: They burned his house down.

Harry: What do you call a lion tamer who sticks
his right arm down a lion's throat?
Garry: I dunno. What?
Harry: Lefty!

She stood on the bridge at midnight,
Her lips were all a-quiver.
She gave a cough; her leg fell off
And floated down the river.

ROTTEN RHYMES

Little Jack Horner
Sat in his corner
Eating his cold meat pie.
He caught salmonella,
Unfortunate fella,
And now is likely to die.

Piggy on the railway, picking up stones.
Along came a train and broke poor Piggy's
bones.
"Hey," said Piggy, "that's not fair!"
"Tough," said the driver, "I don't care!"

_____

During dinner at the Ritz
Aunty May had forty fits
And — which made my sorrow greater —
I was left to tip the waiter.

_____

Mary had a little lamb —
You've heard it all before.
But then she asked for seconds,
And had a little more.

_____

Little Miss Muffet
Sat on a tuffet
Eating her Irish stew.
Along came a spider
And sat down beside her,
So Miss Muffet ate him too.

THE RAINDROPS MAKE THINGS BEAUTIFUL, THE GRASS AND FLOWERS TOO, IF RAIN CAN MAKE THINGS BEAUTIFUL, WHY DOESN'T IT RAIN ON YOU?

UH!

Here lies the body of Senator Key,
Who promised everything to you and me.
His promises he never did fulfill,
And now the fibber's dead — and lying still!

My girlfriend in the mountains
is very shy and meek.
She always dresses in the dark
In case the mountains peek!

Romeo and Juliet,
In a restaurant they met.
He had no cash to pay the debt,
So Romeo'd what Juliet!

There's a peanut sitting on the railway track,
His heart is all a-flutter.
The train comes roaring round the bend —
Toot! toot! — peanut butter.

Up with School

A true story: The school board official was picking his way carefully across the schoolyard one winter day. After several days of hard frost there was a light coating of snow, and the ground was treacherous. Suddenly his legs shot from under him and the official, briefcase and hat went flying. A small boy ran up to him. "Thank you, Sir!" he shouted.

"What do you mean — thank you?" demanded the official.

"You've found our slide!"

Why is the school basketball court always so soggy?

Because the players are always dribbling.

Harry: I don't think my woodshop teacher likes me much.

Garry: What makes you think that?

Harry: He's teaching me to make a coffin!

Teacher: If I had fifty apples in my right hand and thirty apples in my left hand, what would I have?

Debby: Big hands.

Teacher: Can you make a sentence with the word "fascinate" in it?

Debby: My Dad's vest has nine buttons but he can only fascinate.

Teacher: You missed school yesterday, Debby, didn't you?

Debby: No, sir — I didn't miss it one bit!

GIVE ME A SENTENCE WITH THE WORD JUDICIOUS IN IT!

THE HANDS THAT JUDICIOUS CAN BE SOFT AS YOUR FACE.

Harry: Mom, I'm too tired to do my homework.

Mum: Don't be silly — hard work never killed anyone yet.

Harry: But why should I risk being the first?

Teacher: You mustn't fight, Harry. You should learn to give and take.

Harry: I did, sir. He took my Mars bar and I gave him a black eye!

Garry: I is . . .

Teacher: No, Garry. You must say "I am".

Garry: All right. I am the ninth letter of the alphabet.

Teacher: Where are the Andes, Debby?
Debby: At the end of the armies, Ma'am.

"Now, children," said the principal as the school party prepared to board the ferry, "What do you shout if one of the boys falls into the sea?"
Up went Sam's hand. "Boy overboard!" he said.
"Good boy — now what do you shout if one of the teachers falls into the sea?"
"Depends which teacher it is, Sir."

Teacher: What do you know about the Dead Sea?
Garry: I didn't even know it was ill?

Harry: How do you like school, Garry?
Garry: Preferably closed!

Why did the boy take a hammer to school?
He wanted to break up the class.

What car should you take to pick up Chinese food?
A Rolls Rice.

How do you keep a dog from barking in the back seat of a car?
Let him ride in front.

"This car has had one careful owner, sir," said the salesman.
"But it's covered with dents and scratches!"
"I'm afraid the other owners weren't so careful."

There's a cheapo car — let's call it a Plonka — which has given rise to a lot of jokes. Here are just a few of them . . .

What is a Plonka owner's great ambition?
To get a speeding ticket.

Why is a Plonka like a baby?
It never goes anywhere without a rattle.

What's a broken window in a Plonka called?
Air conditioning.

What's a sunroof in a Plonka called?
A small leak.

What do you call a turbo-charged Plonka?
A lawnmower.

TRAVELERS TALES

Stan: In China I saw a woman hanging from a tree.
Dan: Shanghai?
Stan: No, just a few feet off the ground.

———————————

A giant American car pulled up in a sleepy English village.
"Say, am I on the right road for Shakespeare's house?" the driver asked a local yokel.
"Straight ahead," replied the yokel, "but there's no need to hurry — he's dead."

Garry: When we were at the beach a crab bit off one of Dad's toes!
Harry: Which one?
Garry: Dunno. All crabs look alike to me!

———————————

What do they use to count monkeys in Africa?
An ape recorder.

———————————

"I've never flown before," said the nervous old lady to the air hostess. "Your pilot will bring me down safely, won't he?"
"Of course, Madam — he's never left anybody up there yet!"

What will they do when the Forth Bridge collapses?
Build a fifth bridge.

Dan: A friend of mine decided to travel to Paris by train because of his fear of flying. But he was out of luck.
Stan: What happened?
Dan: His train crashed. A plane fell on it.

Dan: I once traveled all the way from New York to Washington and it didn't cost me a penny!
Stan: How did you manage that?
Dan: I walked.

Mr. and Mrs. Brown were arriving at the airport,
ready to take off for their vacation in Greece.
"I wish I'd brought the piano," said Mr. Brown
suddenly.
"Whatever for?"
"I left our tickets on it."

What has twenty-two legs and goes crunch?
A football team eating chips.

Dan: My wife's gone to the West Indies.
Stan: Jamaica?
Dan: No, it was her idea.

The French hitch-hiker was thrilled when the car
pulled up alongside him.
"Want a lift, friend?" asked the driver.
"Oui, oui!" said the hitch-hiker excitedly.
"Not in my car you don't!" said the driver.

AMPHIBIOUS ANTICS

WHAT DO YOU CALL A FROG SPY?

A CROAK AND DAGGER AGENT.

What's green and turns red at the flick of a switch?
A frog in a blender.
That's sick!
So was Mom when she found the blender.

What happens when your pet frog breaks down?
He gets toad away.

What's a frog's favorite sweet?
Lollihops.

What goes Croak! Croak! when it's foggy?
A froghorn.

What's green and goes dah-dit, dah-dah, dah-dit?
Morse toad.

What is a frog's favorite drink?
Croaka-cola.

What is green and white and hops?
A frog sandwich.

JUNGLE JOKES

What do you call a gorilla with a machine-gun?
Sir!

What do you do if there's a gorilla in your bed?
Sleep in the spare room.

Where does Tarzan get his loin-cloths?
From a jungle sale.

HMM, NICE.

What were Tarzan's last words?
Who greased that vine?

What's black and white and very noisy?
A zebra with a drum kit.

What goes around the jungle grunting and putting
all the other animals to sleep?
A wild bore.

What do you call an alligator's telephone?
A rep-dial.

The mighty lion was stalking proudly through the jungle when he spotted a tiny mouse. Drawing himself up to his full height, the lion stared down at the mouse.

The same lion was in the habit of throwing his weight around. "Who is King of the Jungle?" he demanded, knocking a monkey off his branch with one sweep of his powerful paw.
"You are, mighty Lion," replied the monkey.
"Who is King of the Jungle?" the lion asked a hyena in a voice full of menace.
"You are, mighty Lion," answered the hyena at once.
Presently the lion met an elephant, "Who is King of the Jungle?" he demanded. The elephant did not reply. Instead he picked up the lion in his powerful trunk and threw him into a patch of thorns.
"All right, all right!" muttered the lion.
"No need to get nasty just because you don't know the answer!"

How do you stop a skunk from smelling?
Hold his nose.

How many ears did Captain Kirk have?
Three — a left ear, a right ear and a final frontier.

What do astronauts call sausages?
Unidentified Frying Objects.

Why did Mickey Mouse take a trip to outer space?
He wanted to find Pluto.

Where do astronauts leave their cars?
At parking meteors.

What did the astronaut find in his stocking at Christmas?
Missile-toe.

When do astronauts eat?
At launch time.

What do astronauts play in their spare time?
Star Tac Toe.

Two astronauts knocked on the Pearly Gates.
St. Peter opened them.
"Come in, gentlemen," he said, "and make yourselves comfortable while I check your records."
"Oh, we don't want to come in, thank you," said the first astronaut.
"You don't want to come to heaven!" exclaimed St. Peter. "What do you want then?"
"Please, sir," said the second astronaut, "may we have our space capsule back?"

How do you put a baby astronaut to sleep?
Rocket.

How do you make a Maltese cross?
Step on his toes.

How do Vikings send secret messages?
They use Norse code.

How do you make a Swiss roll?
Push him down the hill.

How do you make a Venetian blind?
Rub soap in his eyes.

I'M TERRIBLY SORRY FOR HITTING YOUR DOG — OF COURSE I'LL REPLACE HIM.

THANK YOU. HOW GOOD ARE YOU AT CATCHING RATS?

What did Richard drive in China?
A Rickshaw.

The trainee pilot was in trouble. He radioed for help.
"Mayday! Mayday!" he gasped. "My engines are on fire!"
The voice from the control tower was calm and business-like.
"Please state your height and position."
"I'm five foot ten and I'm sitting in the cockpit — now please send help!"

Why do Eskimos live on whale meat and blubber?
You'd cry too if all you had was whale meat.

—————

Some places have better bus services than others.
A man in the USA received $100,000
compensation after he was run over by a bus.
"This is an easy way to make money," he thought.
After he got out of hospital he went to France,
where he stood at a bus stop with his leg sticking
out. Soon a bus came along and ran over his leg
. . . 500,000 francs compensation.
As soon as he was well again, the man went to
London and tried the same trick. There he stood
at the Number 9 bus stop with his leg sticking out
into the road . . . He died of pneumonia.

—————

Dan and Stan were driving through New York.
Stan was getting worried about his friend's
driving.
"Dan," he asked, "Why do you always close your
eyes whenever there's a red light?"
"Well," said Dan, "when you've seen one, you've
seen them all!"

—————

Why is Europe like a frying pan?
Because it has Greece at the bottom.

—————

Where do you always need an overcoat?
Chile.

Which country has the best appetite?
Hungary.

What country hates Thanksgiving?
Turkey.

A traveller stopped outside a monastery and asked for shelter for the night. He was shown to a small bare room by a friendly monk.
"Supper will be in half an hour," the monk told him.
The traveller went down to the refectory, expecting something very frugal — cabbage soup and bread and water, perhaps. Instead, he was given a huge plate of crispy fried cod and a huge helping of chips.
"This is the best supper I've ever had," he told the monk sitting next to him. "Who does the cooking?"
"Well, Brother Dominic is our chip monk and Father Peter is the chief friar."

Cabby — how much will it cost to take me to the station?"
"A fiver."
"How much for my suitcase?"
"No charge."
"OK then — you take my suitcase to the station, and I'll walk!"

NIFTY NAMES

What do you call a man who comes through your mailbox?
Bill.

_____

What do you call a man who loves fishing?
Rod.

_____

What do you call a woman who balances glasses of root beer on her nose?

BEATRIX

What do you call a man hanging on the wall?
Art.

_____

What do you call a man with a shovel?
Doug.

_____

What do you call a man who's lost his shovel?
Douglas.

_____

What do you call a man who's been buried in a bog for twenty years?

PETE

The doctor was very good at dealing with patients who telephoned at night. His answer was always: "Take two aspirins and call me in the morning." One evening, however, he was very distressed to find that his toilet wouldn't flush. At once he called the plumber, who listened carefully to the doctor's description of the problem.

"Do you have any aspirins, Doctor?" asked the plumber at last.

"Yes, of course."

"Well, drop two of them down the toilet and if that doesn't work, call me in the morning!"

DOCTOR, DOCTOR, I'VE SWALLOWED A WRENCH!

ARE YOU CHOKING?

NO, I'M SERIOUS.

How's the little boy who swallowed the silver dollar, doctor?
No change yet, I'm afraid.

Doctor, doctor, everyone keeps ignoring me.
Next please!

Doctor, doctor, I feel like an old sock.
Well, I'll be darned.

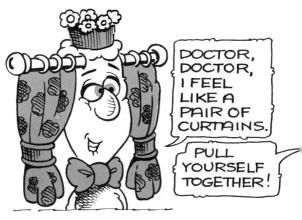

Doctor, doctor, I feel like a deck of cards.
I'll deal with you later.

Doctor, doctor, I feel like a spoon.
Sit still and don't stir.

Doctor, doctor, I can't get to sleep.
Sit on the edge of the bed and you'll soon drop off.

Doctor, doctor, will you give me something for my kidneys?
How about this nice side of bacon?

Doctor, doctor, I can't stop shoplifting!
I'll give you something to take for it.

Doctor, doctor, I feel like a symphony.
Really, I must make some notes about your case.

Mrs. Smithers, you have acute appendicitis.
I came here to be treated, not admired, Doctor!

Doctor, doctor, I feel like a bell.
Take these pills, and if they don't help give me a ring.

The doctor looked very serious as he laid down his stethoscope.

"I'm sorry to tell you," he began, "that you have rabies."

"Quick!" said his patient. "Give me a pencil and paper!"

"Are you going to write your will?" asked the doctor.

"No — I'm making a list of people I'm going to bite!"

Doctor, doctor! Please can you help me out?
Of course — which way did you come in?

Sarah fell down and broke her wrist. The doctor put it in a cast.

"When this cast comes off," asked Sarah, "will I be able to play the piano?"

"Yes, of course," said the doctor. "Just give that wrist time to heal and your fingers will be dancing over the keys as good as new."

"That's funny," said Sarah. "I couldn't play the piano before!"

Doctor, doctor, I feel like a cricket ball.
How's that?

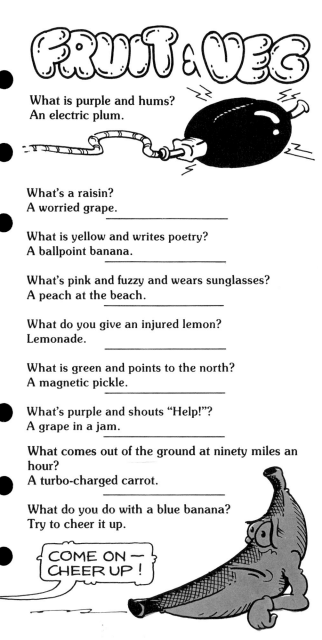

FRUIT & VEG

What is purple and hums?
An electric plum.

What's a raisin?
A worried grape.

What is yellow and writes poetry?
A ballpoint banana.

What's pink and fuzzy and wears sunglasses?
A peach at the beach.

What do you give an injured lemon?
Lemonade.

What is green and points to the north?
A magnetic pickle.

What's purple and shouts "Help!"?
A grape in a jam.

What comes out of the ground at ninety miles an hour?
A turbo-charged carrot.

What do you do with a blue banana?
Try to cheer it up.

COME ON —
CHEER UP!

BEAR NECESSITIES

A family of polar bears were sitting on an iceberg. Mother Bear said, "I have a tale to tell." So she told the story of how the bear got his fur coat.

"I have a tale to tell too," said Father Bear. And he recounted the story of how the bear got his sharp teeth.

Baby Bear shifted uncomfortably on the chilly iceberg. "My tail's *cold*!" he complained.

The Grizzly Bear is fierce and wild.
He has devoured the infant child.
The infant child is unaware
He has been eaten by the bear.

Which bear needs a deodorant?
Pooh Bear.

A jolly old bear at the Zoo
Could always find something to do.
When it bored him to go
On a walk to and fro,
He reversed, and walked fro and to.

WAITER, WAITER!

Waiter, this soup tastes funny.
Then why aren't you laughing, sir?

How did you find your steak, sir?
Quite easily — I moved this french fry aside and
there it was.

Waiter, have you got soup on the menu today?
No, sir, I wiped it off.

Waiter, there's a fly in my soup.
Don't worry, sir, there's a spider on the bread.

Waiter, there's a fly in my soup!
Just a moment, sir — I'll call the Humane
Society!

Waiter, there's a dead fly in my soup.
Oh dear, it's the hot water that kills them.

Yuk — there's a little beetle on my salad!
Sorry, sir, I'll go and fetch you a bigger one.

Waiter, please call the manager. I can't eat this
soup.
He won't want it either, sir.

What do you give a sick canary?
Tweetment.

Why do swallows fly south for the winter?
It's too far to walk.

Why do eagles sit in churches?
Because they are birds of prey.

What's the difference between unlawful and
illegal?
Unlawful is against the law; illegal is a sick bird.

What do you get when you cross a dog with a
chicken?
A hen that lays pooched eggs.

What kind of bird digs for coal?
A mynah bird.

Which bird always succeeds?
A parakeet with no teeth.

What do canaries eat for breakfast?
Tweeties.

Where did Walt Disney get Donald Duck?
Out of a quacker.

What do you get when you cross a woodpecker
with a carrier pigeon?
A bird who knocks before delivering his
message.

Which bird grows up while it grows down?
A baby duckling.

Why do elephants paint their toenails red?
So they can hide in cherry trees without being seen.

Why do elephants wear green felt hats?
So they can walk across pool tables without being noticed.

Why do elephants paint the soles of their feet yellow?
So they can hide upside down in the mustard.

Ever seen an elephant in a cherry tree? or on a pool table? or in a jar of mustard? No? Shows how good the camouflage is!

What's grey and lights up at night?
An electric elephant.

What's grey and has four legs and a trunk?
A mouse going on vacation.

How can you tell an elephant's been in your fridge?
By the smell of peanuts and the footprints in the butter.

How do you get down from an elephant?
You don't get down from an elephant, you get down from a duck.

How does an elephant get down from a tree?
He stands on a leaf and waits for autumn.

Dan: Would you rather have an elephant chase you or a lion?
Stan: I'd rather have it chase the lion!

What do you get if you cross an elephant with a 747 ?
A jumbo jet.

Do you know the difference between a mailbox and an elephant's ear? No?
I'll never send you to mail a letter!

Why do elephants wear sneakers?
To surprise mice.

Stupid SWEETS

What's white and fluffy and swings through the cake shop?
A meringue-utang.

What cake flies through the air and comes back again?
A boomeringue.

What is pink and wobbly and flies?
A Jellocopter.

How do Jellos start their races?
Get set!

The rabbit raced the tortoise,
And the tortoise won the money,
When Mr. Rabbit came in late,
He was a hot cross bunny!

What has brown spots and flies?
A Chocolate spacechip cookie.

And what is yellow and very dangerous?
Shark-infested custard.

What is yellow and a whiz at math?
A banana with a pocket calculator.

How can you make an apple puff?
Chase it around the garden a few times.

Why did the strawberries cry?
Because they were in a jam.

TRAMPS, PREPPIES and YUPPIES

An old tramp stopped a lady in the street.
"Please give me a fiver for a cup of coffee," he begged.
"A cup of coffee doesn't cost $5!" retorted the lady.
"But I'm expecting company!" explained the tramp.

EVERY DAY MY DOG AND I GO FOR A TRAMP IN THE WOODS..

...WE ENJOY IT, BUT THE TRAMP'S GETTING A BIT FED UP!

A Very Important Person came to the Smith's house one evening. Young Peter brought him a glass of sherry, then stood around watching the guest's every move.
Finally Peter said, "Please will you do your trick now?"
"What trick?" asked the puzzled VIP.
"Well, my Dad says you drink like a fish!"

"Harry, call 911! There's a horrible old tramp in the kitchen and he's eating my home-made buns!"
"Which shall I ask for, dear? Police or ambulance?"

How many yuppies does it take to change a light bulb?
Three — one to get the Rolodex, one to call the electrician and one to pour the gin and tonics.

The dirty old tramp was standing in the street playing a harmonica very badly.
"Please, kind sir," said the tramp to a passer-by, "Have you got a dollar for something to eat?"
"No," said the passer-by.
"Well, have you got a quarter for a cup of coffee?"
"No," said the passer-by.
"Gee-whiz," said the tramp. "You're worse off than I am. Here — you'd better take my harmonica!"

The same tramp knocked at the back door of a house and asked for something to eat.

"What — are you here again?" exclaimed the lady of the house. "I gave you a piece of my home-made pie yesterday!"

"That's right, lady," said the tramp, "but I'm OK now!"

Nigel the yuppie was driving along in his BMW listening to his CD player, with his right arm hanging out of the window. Suddenly a car going in the opposite direction veered out to avoid a bicyclist and scraped the BMW's side. Nigel called for help on his carphone. Soon the police arrived, to find Nigel in tears beside his damaged car.

"My beautiful car!" he wailed.

"Never mind the car," said the policeman, "You've hurt your arm."

Nigel glanced down at his mangled right arm and started to cry again.

"My watch!" he sobbed. "My lovely Rolex wristwatch!"

GHASTLY GIGGLES

Why do witches ride on broomsticks?
They can't afford vacuum cleaners.

Did you hear about the stupid ghost?
He climbed over walls!

What boats do vampires like?
Blood vessels.

Where do ghosts get their jokes?
They have a crypt writer.

Who writes jokes about spooks?
A ghost writer.

How do you flatten a ghost?
Use a spirit level.

What do monsters have for breakfast?
Dreaded wheat.

What's Dracula's favorite place in New York?
The Vampire State Building.

What do you call a handsome, lovable monster?
A total failure.

What do ghosts eat for lunch?
Ghoulash.

Who looks after spooks on airplanes?
Air ghostesses.

What did the vampire say to his victim?
Fangs for the memories.

What do you call a play that's acted by ghosts?
A phantomime.

What do vampire doctors say?
Necks, please!

Mommy, what's a vampire?
Shut up and eat your soup before it clots!

IF YOU WANT
TO JOIN MY
FAN CLUB
SEND YOUR
NAME, ADDRESS
AND BLOOD TYPE

THANKS – BUT NO THANKS

There's a man at the door with a wooden leg.
Tell him to skip it.

There's a man at the door with a bill.
It's probably a duck.

There's a man at the door with an old baby
carriage.
Tell him to push off.

There's a man at the door collecting for the new
school swimming pool.
Give him a glass of water!

There's a man at the door selling beehives.
Tell him to buzz off.

There's a man at the door with a mustache.
Tell him I've already got one.

THERE'S A MAN AT THE DOOR COLLECTING FOR THE OLD PEOPLE'S HOME. SHALL I GIVE HIM GRANDPA?